Succeeding with the Master
THE FESTIVAL COLLECTION®

Compiled and edited by HELEN MARLAIS

About the Series

Welcome to *The Festival Collection*®! This eight-volume series is designed to give students and teachers a great variety of fabulous repertoire from the Baroque, Classical, Romantic, and Twentieth/Twenty-First Centuries. The series is carefully leveled from elementary through advanced repertoire. These pieces are true crowd pleasers and will showcase students' technical and musical abilities. Each level covers the gamut of your repertoire needs, from works that showcase power and bravura, to pieces that develop a student's sense of control and finesse. Having a wide selection of works with pedagogically-correct leveling will help make your repertoire selections easier and your students' performances more successful.

Each book includes a CD recording of all of the corresponding works to guide students in their interpretation. The editing in the scores reflects these CD performances. While the CD performances are consistent with the editing in the books, and vice versa, they also demonstrate an appropriate degree of interpretive license. My goal is to instill an appreciation for accurate performances, while nurturing a sense for stylistically appropriate interpretive license. Books one through six were recorded by Helen Marlais, and books seven and eight were recorded by Helen Marlais, Chiu-Ling Lin, and Frances Renzi, giving students at these higher levels the opportunity to hear three different performance styles.

The Festival Collection® is a companion series to the *Succeeding with the Masters*® series. *Succeeding with the Masters*® provides the student with practice strategies and valuable information about the musical characteristics of each era. *The Festival Collection*® expands the repertoire selection with numerous additional top-drawer pedagogical works in a wide array of styles, and with different musical and technical demands. There is no duplication of repertoire between these two series. All of the pieces in both series are motivational and exciting for students to learn as well as for teachers to teach!

Enjoy the series!

THE FJH MUSIC COMPANY INC.
Frank J. Hackinson

Production: Frank J. Hackinson
Production Coordinators: Joyce Loke and Philip Groeber
Cover Design and Art Direction: Gwen Terpstra, Terpstra Design, San Francisco, CA,
Cover Art Concept: Helen Marlais
Illustration: Keith Criss, TradigitalWorks, Oakland, CA
Engraving: Tempo Music Press, Inc.
Printer: Tempo Music Press, Inc.

ISBN-13: 978-1-56939-595-0

The Festival Collection® Book 7

The Festival Collection® Book 7

ALLEMANDE

from *French Suite No. 1, BWV 812*

Johann Sebastian Bach
(1685-1750)

SARABANDE

from *French Suite No. 1, BWV 812*

Johann Sebastian Bach
(1685-1750)

ALLEGRO

from *Suite No. 7, HWV 432*

George Frideric Handel
(1685-1759)

ALLEMANDE

from *French Suite No. 4, BWV 815*

Johann Sebastian Bach
(1685-1750)

GIGA

from *Sonata in D major*

Baldassare Galuppi
(1706-1785)

SINFONIA NO. 6

(BWV 792)

Johann Sebastian Bach
(1685-1750)

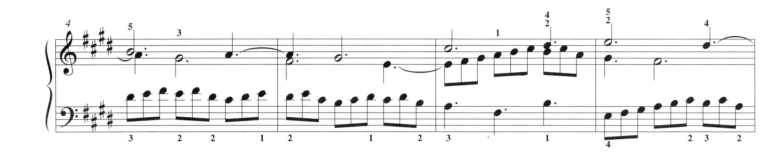

N.B. The appoggiaturas in measures 34 and 41 are editorial.

Prelude No. 4

from *Six Little Preludes, (BWV 936)*

Johann Sebastian Bach
(1685-1750)

SINFONIA No. 15

(BWV 801)

Johann Sebastian Bach
(1685-1750)

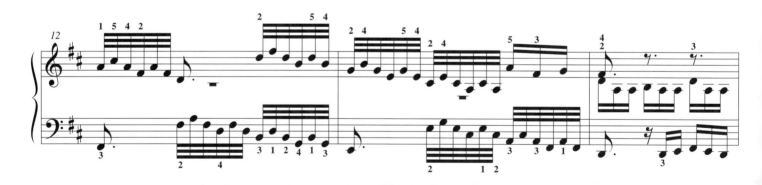

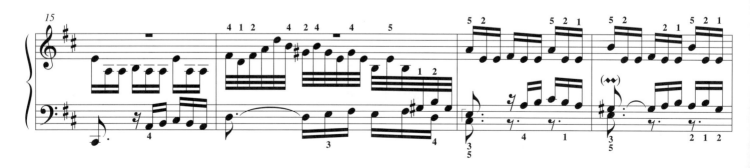

SONATA IN C MAJOR

(K.159/L.104)

Domenico Scarlatti
(1685-1757)

FANTASIE IN D MINOR

(KV 397)

Wolfgang Amadeus Mozart
(1756-1791)

SONATA IN G

(KV 283, First Movement: Allegro)

Wolfgang Amadeus Mozart
(1756-1791)

MOONLIGHT SONATA

(Sonata No. 14, Opus 27, No. 2, First Movement)

Ludwig van Beethoven
(1770-1827)

sempre pianissimo e senza sordini

con pedale

dédiée á Madame Duvivier

SONATA IN B FLAT MAJOR

(Air du ballet de Mirza avec des variations, Oeuvre 1, No. 2, Third Movement)

Muzio Clementi
(1752-1832)

SONATA IN E MINOR

(Hob. XVI/34, Third Movement)

Franz Joseph Haydn
(1732-1809)

44

Sonata in C major

(KV 545, First Movement)

Wolfgang Amadeus Mozart
(1756-1791)

VARIATIONS IN G MAJOR
from *Six Easy Variations, WoO 77*

Ludwig van Beethoven
(1770-1827)

Theme

Andante, quasi allegretto ($\quarternote$ = 56-63)

Variation 1

Variation 2

Variation 3

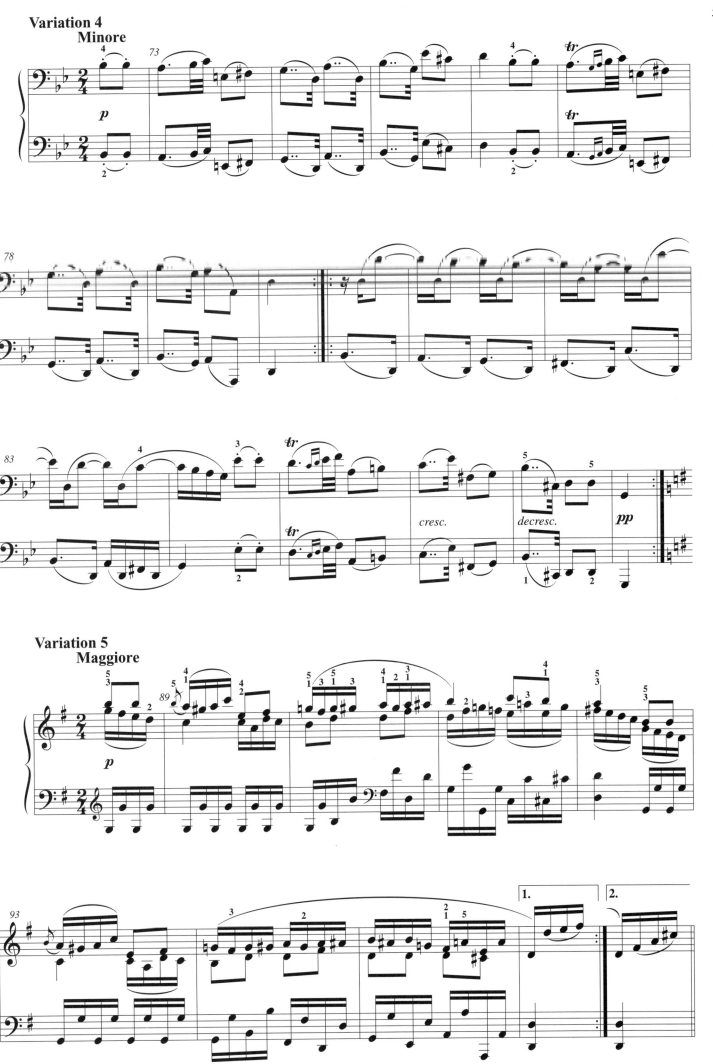

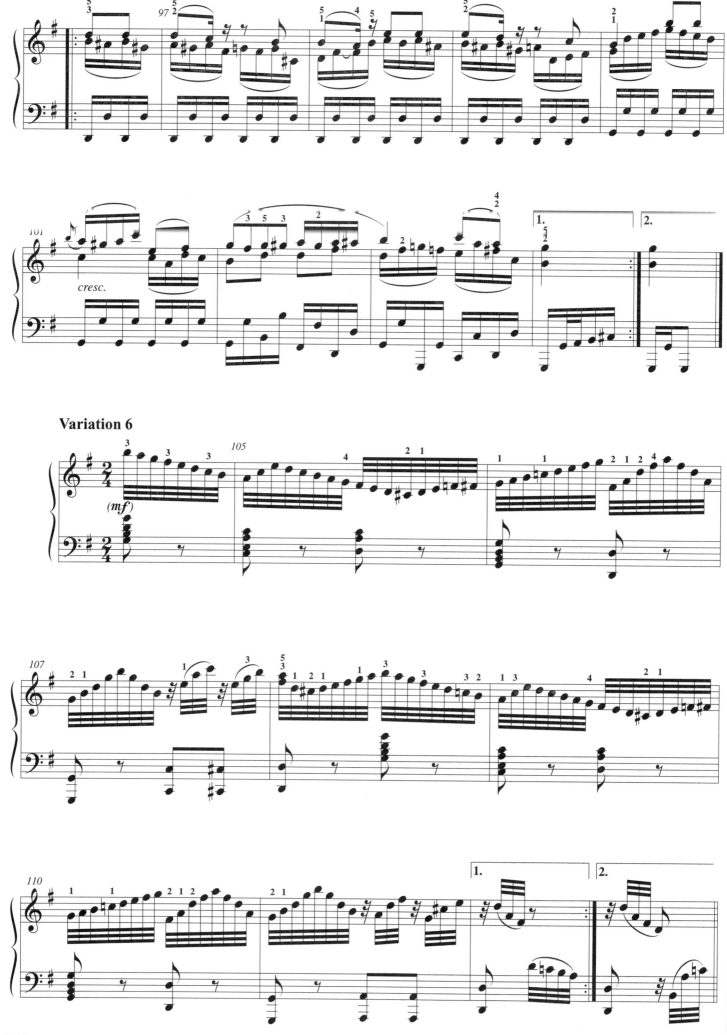

Variation 6

MOMENTS MUSICAUX

(Opus 94, No. 3, D.780)

Franz Schubert
(1797-1828)

Allegro moderato

TWO WALTZES

Johannes Brahms
(1833-1897)

Opus 39, No. 3

Opus 39, No. 4

WALTZ IN A FLAT MAJOR

(Opus 70, No. 2)

Frédéric Chopin
(1810-1849)

* The first note and the C should be played together.

ROMANZE

(Opus 28, No. 2)

Robert Schumann
(1810-1856)

THE BAMBOULA

(African Dance, Opus 59, No. 8)

Samuel Coleridge-Taylor
(1875-1912)

APRIL

from *The Seasons, Opus 37b, No. 4*

Pyotr Ilyich Tchaikovsky
(1840-1893)

FJH1591

Notturno
from *Lyric Pieces, Opus 54, No. 4*

Edvard Grieg
(1843-1907)

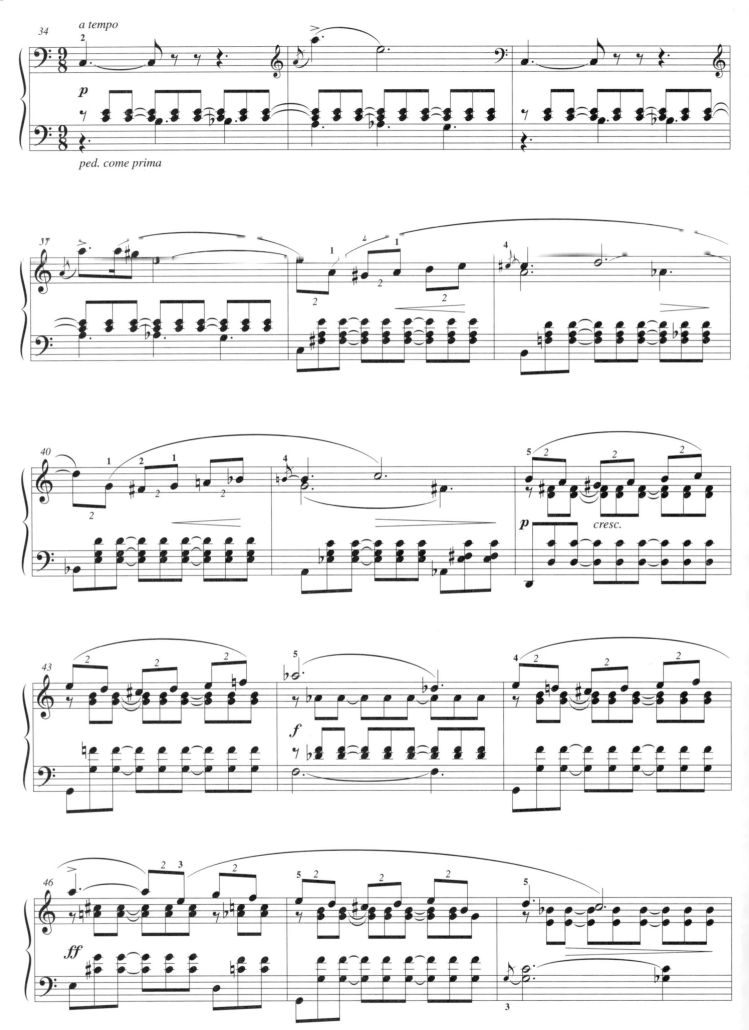

TARANTELLA

Albert Pieczonka
(19th Century)

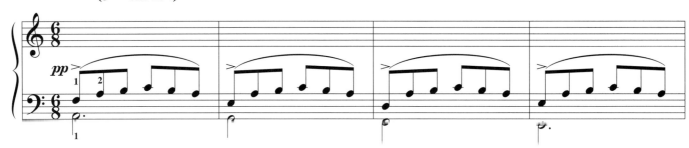

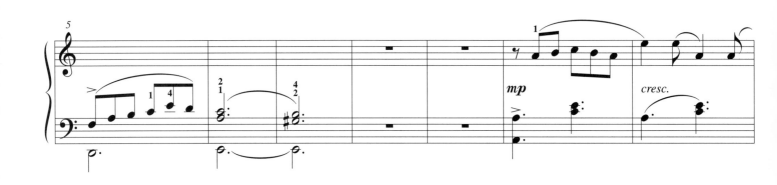

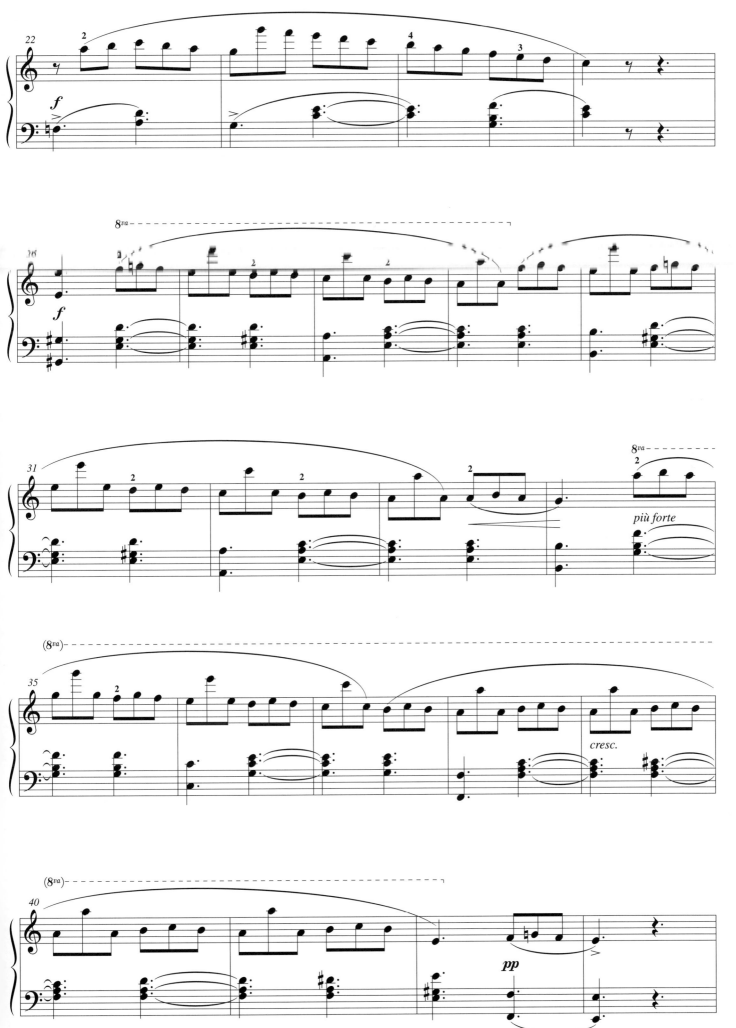

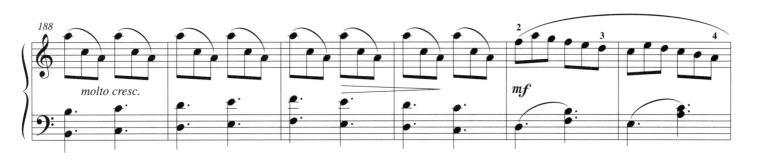

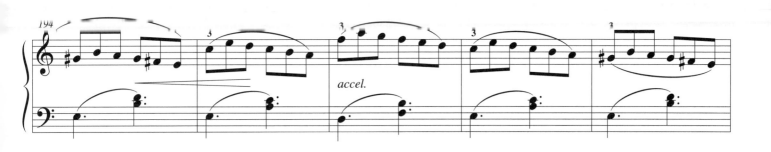

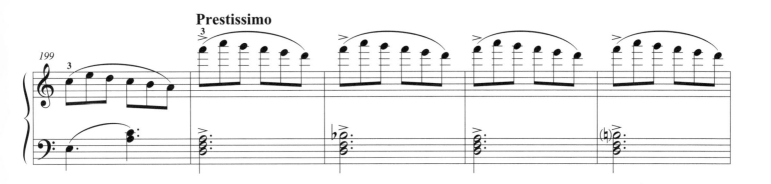

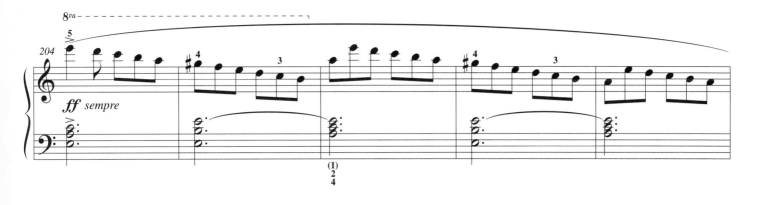

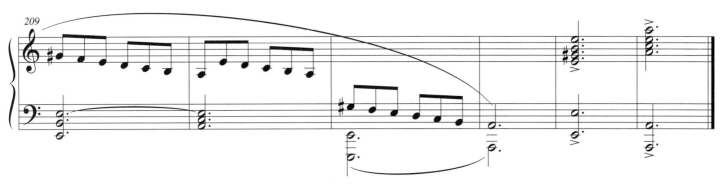

FJH1591

FOREST BIRDS

Waldvöglein, from *Idyllen, Opus 43*

Adolf Jensen
(1837-1879)

Lebhaft und leicht (Lively and light)

VENETIAN BOAT SONG

(Opus 30, No. 6)

Felix Mendelssohn
(1809-1847)

Allegretto tranquillo (♩. = 56-63)

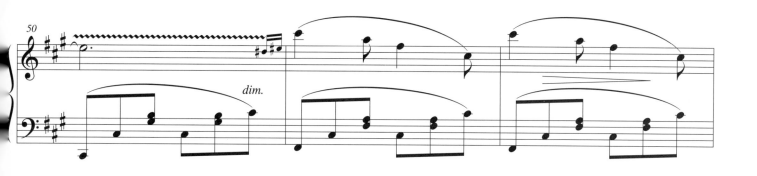

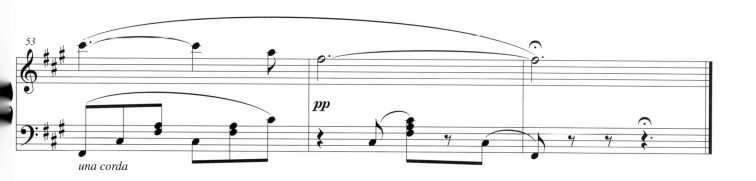

STUDY IN D MINOR

(Warrior's Song, Opus 45, No. 15)

Stephen Heller
(1813-1888)

O POLICHINELLO

from *A Próle do Bébé, Suite No. 1*

Heitor Villa-Lobos
(1887-1959)

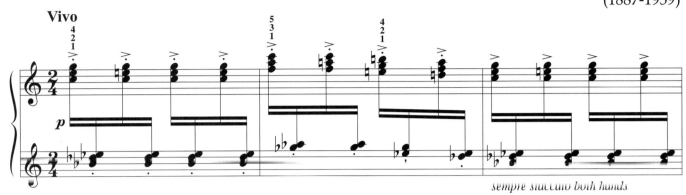

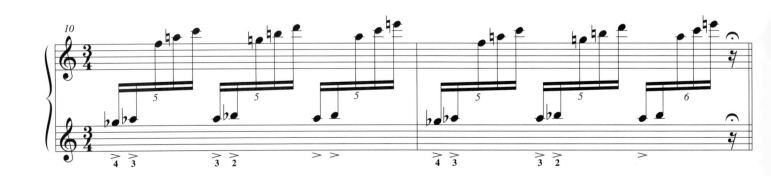

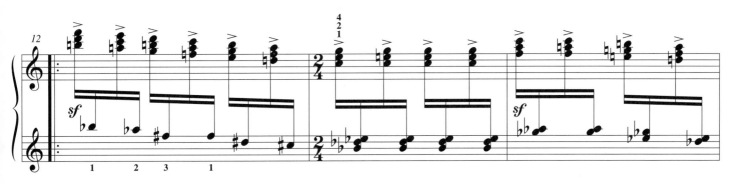

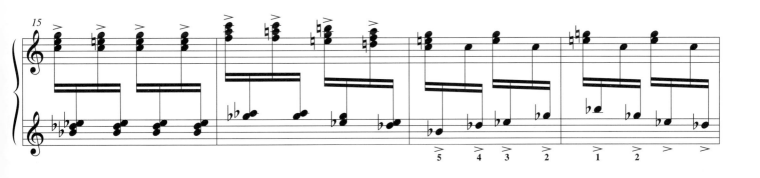

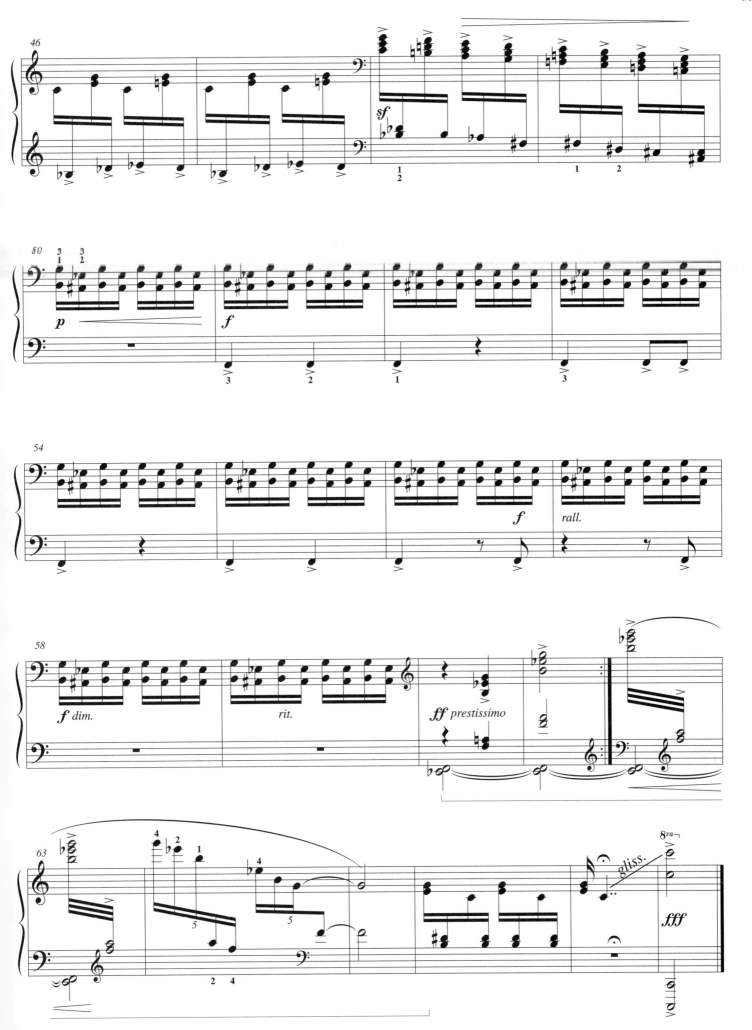

GALOP FINAL

from *11 Pezzi infantili*

Alfredo Casella
(1883-1947)

Fantastic Dance No. 1

from *Three Fantastic Dances, Opus 5*

Dmitri Shostakovich
(1906-1975)

PLAYERA

from *Danzas españolas, Opus 5, No. 5*

Enrique Granados
(1867-1916)

CRIS DANS LA RUE

from *Scènes d'enfants*

Federico Mompou
(1893-1987)

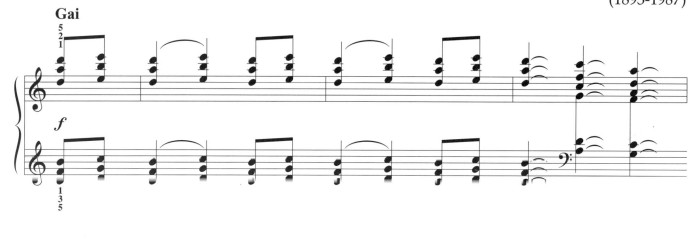

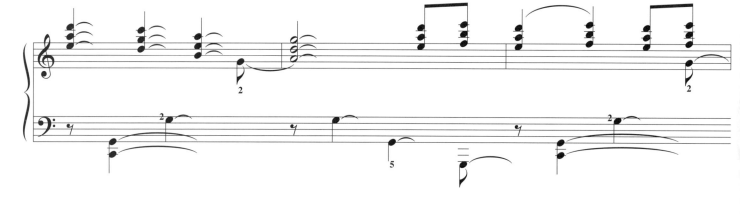

Gai lointain

FIRST ARABESQUE

Claude Debussy
(1862-1918)

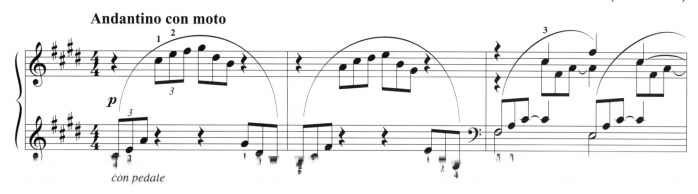

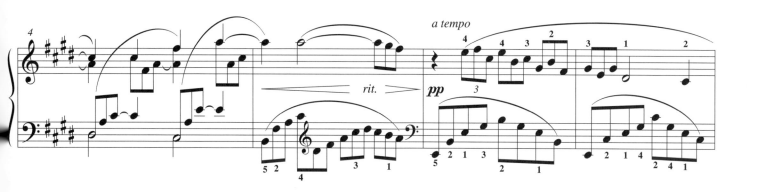

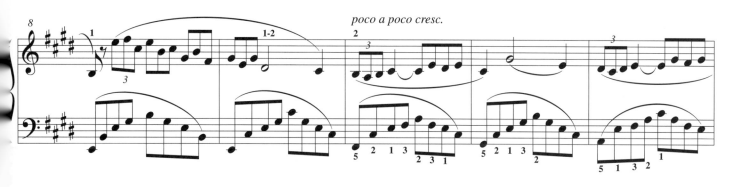

Tempo rubato

Sonatina in C major for Piano

(First Movement)

Aram Ilyich Khachaturian
(1903-1978)

a tempo (poco tranquillo)

ABOUT THE PIECES AND THE COMPOSERS

BAROQUE ERA

Allemande (from *French Suite No. 1, BWV 812*), by Johann Sebastian Bach (1685-1750)
The *suite* was a significant musical form during the Baroque era. The earliest suites, dating back to the fourteenth century, took the form of the pairing of dances. In time the number of dances increased until the suite became a potpourri of international dance types: the German *allemande*, the French *courante*, the Spanish *sarabande*, and the English *gigue*, or jig. Bach wrote six French suites, which were composed between 1722 and 1725. The first five appear in their original versions in the *Clavierbüchlein* for Anna Magdalena Bach.

Sarabande (from *French Suite No. 1, BWV 812*), by Johann Sebastian Bach (1685-1750)
The short movements of the Baroque suites, characterized by dance rhythm, were usually composed in the same key, conforming to one another in theme. Bach wrote most of his suites for the harpsichord — the *allemande* in quadruple time, the *courante* in moderate triple, the *sarabande* in slow triple meter, and the lively *gigue*. Sometimes he inserted a minuet or gavotte, or a bourrée or a passepied, which are dances that could add richness to the formality of the suite form.

Allegro (from *Suite No. 7, HWV 432*), by George Frideric Handel (1685-1759)
Allegro, the Italian word for "lively," is also used to denote a fast movement in a piece of music. This allegro is the third movement in Handel's *Suite No. 7*, first published in 1720. Like several other Baroque musical forms, the suite reached its peak as an art form in the works of Bach and Handel. Except for his famous orchestral suites *Water Music* and *Music for the Royal Fireworks*, Handel seems to have restricted his suites to the keyboard. The best-known examples of Baroque orchestral suites are Handel's *Water Music* and four suites written by Bach.

Allemande (from *French Suite No. 4, BWV 815*), by Johann Sebastian Bach (1685-1750)
The *allemande* is a stately dance from Germany whose earliest reference can be dated back to the sixteenth century in a dancing manual published in London. In the seventeenth and eighteenth centuries, as the first movement of the baroque suite, it was altered significantly. It became formalized, and was characterized by two running melodies. The harpsichord suite occasionally opened with a prelude. In addition to his set of French suites, Bach composed a set of six English suites during his last few years in Weimar and first few years in Cöthen.

Giga (from *Sonata in D major*), by Baldassare Galuppi (1706-1785)
The Italian composer, conductor, and instrumentalist Baldassare Galuppi was born in Burano, near Venice. Well known as a musician, he bore the nickname "Il Buranello," after the town of his birth. His father, a barber by trade, was a violinist in small orchestras that played between acts of Venetian spoken comedies, and he taught his son music. Baldassare composed his first opera at the age of sixteen, and after excelling as a student of keyboard and composition, he had a brilliant career as a significant contributor to the development of the *opera buffa*, a type of comic opera. *Giga* is the Italian term for jig or gigue.

Sinfonia No. 6 *(BWV 792)*, by Johann Sebastian Bach (1685-1750)
During the Baroque era, musicians like Bach and Handel were daringly creative. The result was that they developed musical forms in new ways. Bach used the name *sinfonia* for his three-part inventions. This was an unusual and creative use of the term, as the original meaning for this Italian word was "symphony." Bach's inventions, however, were written for the clavier, i.e. a keyboard instrument, and are melodic exercises with themes that, though they may be very different, are naturally suited to one another.

Prelude No. 4 *(BWV 936)*, by Johann Sebastian Bach (1685-1750)
Johann Sebastian was the most important member of the Bach family. His keyboard virtuosity earned him almost legendary renown during his lifetime, and his compositional skills earned him a place in history as a master composer.

Orphaned at an early age, Bach lived with his elder brother and began to compose music as a boy. As an adult he lived and worked in a number of cities. He spent many important years in Weimar, where as court organist he wrote most of his organ works. In Cöthen, he was in the employ of a musically educated and appreciative prince, and in Leipzig he held the prestigious appointment of Kantor at the Thomasschule, where he involved himself extensively in the composition of church music.

This prelude is from one of his lesser known keyboard collections called *Six Little Preludes*.

Sinfonia No. 15 *(BWV 801)*, by Johann Sebastian Bach (1685-1750)
Part of Bach's virtuosity as a keyboard composer lies in the fact that he understood the differences between the organ and the harpsichord. He was sought out as a teacher in Weimar, and his teaching activities expanded in Leipzig. Keyboard music was his preference in his lessons. He would start with his inventions (which included his sinfonias), move on to his French and English suites, and conclude with more complex works, thereby gradually introducing the widest variety of keyboard technique possible.

Sonata in C major *(K.159/L.104)*, by Domenico Scarlatti (1685-1757)
Born in the same year as Bach and Handel, Domenico Scarlatti was the son of Alessandro Scarlatti, a prolific composer of operas, masses, and cantatas. Domenico was one of the most original composers in the history of music. His style is characterized by exceptionally creative use of the keyboard: there are brilliant runs, the crossing of hands, contrasts of low and high register, double notes, trills, and arpeggios. His fame rests on his 500-plus sonatas, and his 30 *Essercizi* or exercises, which he called *Essercizi per gravicembalo*, or "exercises for the harpsichord."

CLASSICAL ERA

Fantasie in D minor *(KV 397)*, by Wolfgang Amadeus Mozart (1756-1791)
In a *fantasie*, fancy is allowed to take precedence over the standard restrictions of structure. These works are improvisational in nature. Mozart's music was an assimilation of Italian, German and French influences, and like Haydn and Beethoven, his music was universally appreciated and is extremely refined. Mozart's joyfulness and sense of humor are evident in many of his compositions.

Sonata in G (*KV 283, First Movement: Allegro*), by Wolfgang Amadeus Mozart (1756-1791)
Mozart achieved mastery in all the forms of his art by the time he reached adulthood. His keyboard sonatas were composed for private concerts and familial, intimate surroundings, unlike his piano concertos, which were written for the concert platform. He often sent sonatas home to his sister Nannerl, as she was also an accomplished musician.

The *Sonata in G (KV 283)* is from a set of five sonatas that were completed during a visit to Munich in 1774 and 1775.

Moonlight Sonata (*Sonata No. 14, Opus 27, No. 2, First Movement*),
by Ludwig van Beethoven (1770-1827)
Beethoven's early sonatas conform to the Viennese Classical model of Mozart and Haydn. As the sonata moved from the salon to the public concert hall, Beethoven expanded the form. The *Moonlight Sonata* was written in C sharp minor for piano in 1801. Beethoven referred to it as a "sonata in the style of a fantasia," and it was published in Vienna in 1802 as *Quasi una Fantasia.* Ludwig Rellstab, a German music critic, is said to be the first to draw a comparison between the first movement and moonlight on Lake Lucerne in Switzerland.

Sonata in B flat major (*Air du ballet de Mirza avec des variations, Oeuvre 1, No. 2, Third Movement*),
by Muzio Clementi (1752-1832)
Born in Italy, Muzio Clementi went to London to study, and sometime between 1775 and 1779 became conductor at the King's Theatre in London. He made a tour of Europe as a virtuoso pianist from which he returned to settle in London. There he became a highly regarded composer, performer, teacher, music publisher, and piano manufacturer. He influenced Beethoven, and he has had a lasting historical influence as a pianist, piano teacher, and composer with his compositions and his teaching works. In 1801 he wrote *The Art of Playing on the Piano-Forte,* which is still in use.

Sonata in E minor (*Hob. XVI:34, Third Movement*), by Franz Joseph Haydn (1732-1809)
Born into the patronage system for artists, Haydn was employed in 1761 by Prince Esterházy, and remained in full employment with this wealthy family until 1790. He met Mozart in 1783 or 1784, and each held the other in very high esteem. He taught Beethoven from 1792 to early 1794. Haydn was directly responsible for the establishment of the string quartet. The classical form of the sonata was simple, with two sections, each repeated. Haydn, like Mozart and Beethoven, expanded the form.

Sonata in C major (*KV 545, First Movement*), by Wolfgang Amadeus Mozart (1756-1791)
Mozart's *Sonata in C major* was composed in Vienna in 1788. This major work was published posthumously under the title *Sonata Facile,* i.e., "easy sonata." Mozart called it "a little keyboard sonata for beginners," and to this day it is part of the piano student's repertory. It is Mozart's most famous sonata. It contains all the things students need to master: ascending and descending scales for both hands, arpeggios, and trills. This sonata, in reality, is not easy at all! Many professional pianists play it as well.

Variations in G major (from *Six Easy Variations, WoO 77*),
by Ludwig van Beethoven (1770-1827)
Beethoven studied piano, organ, violin, and viola as a boy. He later studied in Vienna with tuition assistance from the Elector of Cologne. After the death of his mother and the steady decline in the health of his father, he returned home and taught music to support his brothers. In 1792 he went back to Vienna to study with Haydn. In time he was supported

by a number of aristocratic patrons. Beethoven's *variations* are modifications of a previously stated theme. Each variation is accomplished by means of ornamentation, altered rhythms or harmony, or other forms of development.

ROMANTIC ERA

Moments musicaux *(Opus 94, No. 3, D.780)*, by Franz Schubert (1797-1828)
Franz Schubert was born near Vienna. He learned the violin from his father, and the piano from an elder brother. At a very early age he loved to spend time immersed in the lyric poets of German Romanticism. When he was only seventeen he put Goethe's verse *Gretchen at the Spinning Wheel* to music. His six "musical moments" were written between 1823 and 1828, and are among Schubert's shorter works for piano. They express the new lyricism of the age, which was marked by spontaneity and the charm of the unexpected.

Waltz in G sharp minor *(Opus 39, No. 3)*, by Johannes Brahms (1833-1897)
This German composer was born in Hamburg and died in Vienna. His music is Romantic in nature, but it displays a Classical sense of order as well. He dominated chamber music in the second half of the nineteenth century to the extent that chamber music became synonymous with conservatism in music. Brahms was a child prodigy. He was trained by highly regarded teachers in Hamburg, and moved to Vienna in 1862, where he achieved worldwide recognition and fame. He composed the *Waltzes, Op. 39* in 1865.

Waltz in E minor *(Opus 39, No. 4)*, by Johannes Brahms (1833-1897)
Throughout his life, Brahms was a friend of Clara Schumann. His attraction to her was at first romantic, but he was of help to her when Robert Schumann died, and she was a help to him later, when he moved to Vienna and she introduced him to her circle of friends. Among Brahms' creative activities was the creation of a women's chorus for which he arranged folksongs and wrote original compositions.

Waltz in A flat major *(Opus 70, No. 2)*, by Frédéric Chopin (1810-1849)
With Chopin, Polish music became internationally influential. He studied at the High School of Music which was located on the grounds of the Warsaw Conservatory. His original harmonies and the influence of folk music soon made him the symbol of Polish nationalism. On a European tour, however, he heard that the Russians had captured Warsaw, so he settled in Paris. Chopin devoted himself almost exclusively to the piano and produced short pieces (mazurkas and waltzes), but he was also a master of complex large-scale works, many of which demand virtuoso technique.

Romanze *(Opus 28, No. 2)*, by Robert Schumann (1810-1856)
Schumann was the son of a well-to-do bookseller and author, and he had a wide literary education as a child. His parents were not musical, but Robert was allowed to take piano lessons at school, and he showed outstanding ability. He pursued studies in law but turned to music, lodging with his piano teacher Wieck, whose younger daughter Clara, a concert pianist, became his wife in 1840. Robert's love of literature and his sensitive, lyrical nature lent itself to expression in such songs as this "romance."

The Bamboula (*African Dance, Opus 59, No. 8*), by Samuel Coleridge-Taylor (1875-1912)
This English composer's father, a doctor, was a native of Sierra Leone. In Croydon, where he was raised by his English mother, he studied the violin and sang in the church choir. His first important composition was a *Te Deum*. A cantata from *'The Song of Hiawatha,'* based on Longfellow's poem centering on the Native American, brought him fame throughout England and the United States. Coleridge-Taylor saw the establishment of the dignity of the black man as part of his mission in life. The *bamboula* is a rhapsodic dance.

April (from *The Seasons, Opus 37b, No. 4*), by Pyotr Ilyich Tchaikovsky (1840-1893)
This Russian composer is known for writing some of the most popular classical pieces in the history of Western music. His music has great emotional appeal, like his famous ballets. From December 1875 to November 1876 Tchaikovsky wrote piano pieces after the months of the year, each with its own descriptive title, and in its own key. He named the collection *Les saisons*, or "The Seasons." *April* is written in the key of B flat major and has the title *"Perce-neige,"* which means to "pierce" or "break an opening in" the snow.

Notturno (from *Lyric Pieces, Opus 54, No. 4*), by Edvard Grieg (1843-1907)
Edvard Grieg, Norway's most important composer, was born and died in Bergen. His mother was the daughter of a provincial governor who ensured that she received the best musical training, which led to her becoming a well-known pianist. She gave her young son his first piano lessons when he was six years old. Grieg married the talented Norwegian singer Nina Hagerup. Influenced and inspired by fellow musicians in search of a national Norwegian music, his compositions show his love of the Norwegian folk idioms. Grieg began his famous *Lyric Pieces*, eight pieces evoking the Norwegian spirit, in 1867. Number 4 is entitled "Elves' Dance."

Tarantella, by Albert Pieczonka (19th century)
Little is known about this composer, including his nationality. His *Tarantella* appears in his *Danses de salon*, a French title. In 1871, there was a performance of his work *The Emperor: Grand fantasie heroique on Die Wacht am Rhein, (The Watch/Guard on the Rhine)*, a German patriotic anthem with origins rooted in historical conflicts with France, for which the reviewer wrote, "… The composer… (whose name is new to us) has produced a good showy Fantasia, which, well played, may successfully stir up the German patriotic feeling, and this is we presume what is principally aimed at."

Forest Birds (*Waldvöglein*, from *Idyllen, Opus 43*), by Adolf Jensen (1837-1879)
This German composer came from a musical family. The great influence in his early works was Schumann, and his mature works show the influences of Chopin and Liszt. He had a gift for the musical expression of emotions. A born lyricist, his songs, especially the late English and Scottish songs and ballads, display his extraordinary ability to set words to music. *Forest Birds* is a piano piece from the work *Idyllen, Op. 43*, which Jensen composed in Breslau in 1873.

Venetian Boat Song (*Opus 30, No. 6*), by Felix Mendelssohn (1809-1847)
This German composer was born in Hamburg into a family of means. He was a gifted prodigy, and worshiped Bach, Mozart, Handel, and Beethoven. He was sought out as a conductor, pianist, organist, organizer of musical events, educator, and composer. He turned the Gewandhaus Orchestra at Leipzig into the finest in Europe, and founded the Conservatory of Leipzig, which set new standards for the training of musicians. Unfortunately all his activities left him with very little time to rest. He suffered from exhaustion and a series of strokes and died at the early age of 38.

Study in D minor *(Warrior's Song, Opus 45, No. 15)*, by Stephen Heller (1813-1888)
This French pianist of Hungarian birth was born into the transitional period between late German Romanticism and French Impressionism. He studied in Budapest before moving to Vienna, where he was introduced to Schubert and Beethoven. Heller published more than 160 piano compositions. His studies, still familiar to pianists, were so well received that he had difficulty gaining recognition for his other works. Heller was a friend of Berlioz, and reviewed music for Schumann's music journal.

20TH/21ST CENTURIES

O Polichinello (from *A Próle do Bébé, Suite No. 1*), by Heitor Villa-Lobos (1887-1959)
The Brazilian composer Heitor Villa-Lobos immersed himself in folk music, traveling throughout the states of Brazil and the Amazon, experimenting in rhythm and harmony. He was a self-taught composer and an astute listener. Artur Rubinstein, whom he met in 1918, promoted him and his music throughout the world, and he achieved international acclaim, "brazilianizing" the European popular music of the time. Villa-Lobos wrote in all genres.

Galop final (from *11 Pezzi infantili*), by Alfredo Casella (1883-1947)
This Italian composer, pianist, and conductor was a pupil of the acclaimed French composer and teacher Gabriel Fauré. He was highly influential in Italian music between the two world wars. He traveled widely in Europe and the United States as a pianist and conductor, and committed himself to modernizing Italian music. *11 Pezzi infantili* are a set of "eleven 'childish' (or 'childlike') pieces," evoking the simplicity of childhood. A *galop* was a dance played in duple time, popular during the nineteenth century.

Fantastic Dance No. 1 (from *Three Fantastic Dances, Opus 5*), by Dmitri Shostakovich (1906-1975)
Shostakovich lived and wrote through the turbulent era of Soviet censorship, and although he outlived Stalin, it was a few years before he expanded out of the guidelines of social realism. His output is extremely varied and includes 15 symphonies, 15 string quartets, five operas, an operetta, six concertos, chamber music, music for piano solo, cantatas and oratorios, ballets, 37 film scores, incidental music, vocal music, and orchestral suites. He is remembered primarily as a composer of symphonies. The *Three Fantastic Dances* were composed between 1920 and 1922, and are among his works for piano.

Playera (from *Danzas españolas, Opus 5, No. 5*), by Enrique Granados (1867-1916)
This Spanish composer and pianist established his reputation in Barcelona by giving piano recitals. He played clubs and cafés, from which he later derived his mazurkas, waltzes, and marches. He became involved with the Catalan modernist movement, and when he broke with it he founded a classical concert society and his own music school, which became an important venue for chamber music. Granados' music is rooted in European traditions blended with elements of traditional Spanish folk music.

Cris dans la rue (from *Scénes d'enfants*), by Federico Mompou (1893-1987)
Mompou was a Spanish composer from the region of Catalonia. In 1911 he was able to
satisfy a longing to go to Paris, possibly with a recommendation from the famed Spanish
composer Enrique Granados. Mompou admired Debussy and was influenced by Satie.
He was fond of popular themes, as in this piece, "Cries (or "Clamor") in the Street"
composed between 1915 and 1918. Mompou mastered a beautiful melancholic sound
and a poetic style. He received national honors from Spain and France.

First Arabesque, by Claude Debussy (1862-1918)
The early life of this French composer was unsettled. His piano teacher, the mother-in-law
of the French poet Verlaine, recognized his talent, and he studied at the Paris Conservatory.
He first appeared as a composer in a concert of his songs and violin pieces in 1883. In
1884 he won the Prix de Rome. His *Arabesques I and II* for piano, written in 1890, are
prime examples of the genre in which the music is highly decorated, and often fanciful.

Sonatina in C major for Piano (*First Movement*), by Aram Khachaturian (1903-1978)
This Armenian composer studied at the Moscow Conservatory, and was an established
composer by the time he graduated. Prokofiev recommended his 1932 *Trio for Clarinet,
Violin, and Piano* for performance in Paris, giving him international exposure. His works
were nationalistic, and he wrote the national anthem of Armenia. Although censored
along with his contemporaries Prokofiev and Shostakovich, he received the Lenin Prize
in 1959. His music reflects the basic values of Soviet social realism, blending his
Armenian regional folk roots with Russian tradition.